POWERFUL

QUOTES

FROM

SANKARA

Typesetting, text editing and title

© 2012 The Freedom Religion Press

www.thefreedomreligionpress.com

www.seeseer.com

ISBN: 978-1-937995-86-7

CONTENTS

INTRODUCTION

Adi (the first) Sankara, also known as Sankaracharya (Sankara the Teacher), was one of the most prominent teachers in the religion the West calls "Hinduism."

Hinduism was in a great decline during the time in which Sri Sankara lived and many view Sri Sankara as having saved and revitalized Hinduism.

Some scholars say that Sri Sankara lived from 788 CE to 820 CE.

The quotes in this book were carefully selected for those who wish to have the Direct Experience of the true Self whose nature is Infinite Eternal Existence-Awareness-Bliss and for those who wish to attain Liberation.

That Direct Experience does not occur in the realm of thought or the intellect.

The words are pointers and what is important is to see what the words are pointing towards.

The quotes are practice instructions. Sometimes the practice is to attempt to see from the viewpoint described.

Read the quotes very slowly and every time you read a quote ask yourself these two questions:

A.   What is the purpose of this quote?

B.   What would I have to do to put this purpose into practice?

Write or record your answers to those questions and then reread your notes or listen to your recording repeatedly and actually put the teachings into practice.

If some of the quotes are more helpful to you than others, circle the number of the quotes you find most helpful. Then reread the circled quotes many times repeatedly.

HERE BEGINS

THREE HUNDRED QUOTES

BY SRI SANKARA

DISCERNING THE SELF

FROM THE NON-SELF

1.   When ignorance, the cause,
will be removed, you will be liberated from
the transmigratory existence
consisting of birth and death.
You will never again feel pain
in the states of waking and dream.

2.   You are the non-transmigratory
Supreme Self,
but you wrongly think that you are one
liable to transmigration. (Similarly),
not being an agent or an experiencer
you wrongly consider yourself to be so.
Again, you are eternal
but mistake yourself to be non-eternal.
This is ignorance.

3.   Devoid of contact with the body
the Self is eternal
and characteristically different from it.

4.   The Self is by nature
free from contact with anything.

5.   The Knower which is the Self
is self-evident.

6.   Not being incompatible with
ignorance, actions do not destroy it;
it is knowledge alone that does it.
Ignorance not being destroyed,
the destruction of desire and aversion
is not possible.
Actions caused by impurities
are sure to follow
when desire and aversion are not removed.
Knowledge alone, therefore, is taught here,
so that liberation may be accomplished.

7.   Accompanied by egoism,
actions are incompatible with Knowledge.
Knowledge is the consciousness
that the Self is changeless.

8.   The natural conviction
on the part of the people
that the Self is not different from the body
arises through ignorance.

9.　A man who has Self-knowledge
has neither egoism
nor a desire for the results of actions.

10.　The consciousness of egoism
(which includes the mistaken identity of
the Self with the body etc.)
has its origin in the intellect
and has for its object
what is based on words only.

11.　The knowledge of one's identity
with the pure Self
that negates the wrong notion
of the identity of the body as the Self
sets a man free
when it becomes as firm as the man's belief
that he is a human being.

12.　The Self seems to be moving
when the intellect moves,
and the Self seems to be at rest
when the intellect is at rest
on account of identification
with the intellect,
like trees appearing to move
in the eyes of those
who are in a moving boat.
Similar is the misconception
about transmigratory existence.

13.   Just as trees are thought to be moving
in a direction opposite
to that of a moving boat by a man in it, so,
transmigratory existence is (wrongly)
thought to belong to the Self
(by a man who has identified himself
with the intellect).

14.   The modifications of the intellect
are pervaded by the reflection of
Consciousness when they appear to exist.
So the Self appears to be identified
with sound etc.
This is the reason people are deluded.

15.   Pure Consciousness
is the universal Self
when the object portion is rejected.

16.   After rejecting the object portion
one should accept the Self as the knower
free from all qualifications.
The ego is the object portion.

17.   The Self is different
from the object portion.

18.   Objects of knowledge
appear to exist in the intellect
as long as the intellect is there
in the waking and dream states;
but none exists in the opposite case (i.e.
when the intellect is merged in deep sleep.)
The knower is always the knower.
Therefore, duality has no existence.

19.   Objects that appear
to come into being
and are capable of being made
objects of knowledge
are as unreal as those
that appear in a dream.
As duality has no (real) existence,
Knowledge is eternal and objectless.

20.   I am by nature
pure and changeless consciousness,
devoid of objects.

21.   Untouched by ignorance,
false conceptions (of possessing a body
etc.) and by actions,
the Self is very pure.

22.   All grief and delusion are removed
from those great souls
when there arises the very pure knowledge
of the non-dual Self.

23.   All beings are by nature
Pure Consciousness.
It is due to ignorance that they appear to be
different from Pure Consciousness.

24.   I am all pervading and changeless
Pure Consciousness.

25.   Just as dreams appear to be true
as long as one does not wake up, so, the
identification of oneself with the body etc.
and the seeming authenticity
of sense-perception etc. in the waking state
continue as long as
there is no Self-knowledge.

26.   As actions have ignorance
for their cause,
there is no hope of attaining immortality
from actions.
As liberation is caused by right Knowledge
(alone),
it does not depend on anything else.

27.   Immortality is free from
fear and destruction.

28.   An ignorant man gets identified
with objects of knowledge
and does not know the Self
which is different from objects.

29.   Pain belongs to one
identifying oneself with the body.
One who does not identify
oneself with the body
is free from pain.

30.   The doership of the Self is false
as it depends on the misconception
of the body being the Self.

31.   The knowledge that one is a doer
is certainly false.

32.   I am without any change or motion.
I am pure, devoid of old age, ever free
and without a second.

33.   There is no vision in Me
as I am without the organ of seeing.
How can there be hearing in Me
who have no auditory organ?
Devoid of the organ of speech,
I have no act of speaking in Me.
How can there be thinking in Me
who have no mind?

34.   Ever free, ever pure, changeless,
immovable, immortal, imperishable
and bodiless, I have no knowledge or
ignorance in Me who am of the nature of
the Light of Pure Consciousness only.

35.   I have no hunger, thirst, grief,
delusion, old age or death
as I am without a body.

36.   Devoid of the organ of touch,
I have no act of touching;
and devoid of the tongue,
I have no sensation of taste.
I never have knowledge or ignorance
because I am of the nature of
eternal Consciousness.

37.   Mental modifications
in the forms of objects of knowledge
produced through the instrumentality of
various organs and also those in the forms
of memory, attachment, etc.,
which are only within the mind,
and also those in the dream state
are witnessed by one
different from all of them.
The Knowledge of the Knower is eternal,
pure, infinite and without a second.

38.   It is through the indiscrimination
between the Self
and the modifications of the mind
(false adjuncts to the Self)
that the Knowledge of the Knower
is wrongly conceived by people
to be impure and transitory.

39. I am without any change,
without a mind, all-pervading
and devoid of a body.

40. He who knows the reality of the Self
becomes successful
in attaining the goal of his life
and becomes perfect.

41. Just as the body going from place to
place seen in a dream is not oneself,
so witnessing the body in the waking state
the Seer is different
from that which is seen.

42. I am the Self of all
as the intellects of all beings
are illumined by Me
who am of the nature of
the Light of Consciousness only.

43. It is the intellect that becomes
the instrument, the object, the agent,
actions and their results in a dream.
It is the same in the waking state also.
The Seer is different from the intellect
(and its objects).

44. As they are susceptible to
appearance and disappearance,
the intellect etc. are not the Self.

45.   The ideas "me" and "mine" are
superimposed on the Self due to ignorance.
They do not exist
when the Self is known to be one only.

46.   He has the truest knowledge
who looks upon the Self as a non-agent
having no connection with actions
and their results
and free from the ideas
of "me" and "mine."

47.   One who looks upon the Self
as an agent of actions
and a knower of objects
is not a knower of the Self.

48.   The Self is always of the nature of
the Light of Pure Consciousness
and hence devoid of ignorance.

49.   Always meditating on the Self,
one has nothing to do with time etc.,
as the Self is in no way connected with
time, space, direction and causation.

50.   The Self is always the same
in all beings
and free from old age, death and fear.

51.   The seer is of a nature
different from that of the seen.

52.   What is called the ego
is not a property of the Self.
The other functions
and impurities of the mind
are not properties of the Self.
The Self is without any impurity.

53.   I am not any one of the elements
separately nor their aggregate;
similarly, I am not any one of the senses
nor their aggregate; for they are objects
and instruments of knowledge respectively.
The knower is different from all these.

54.   The sun does not require
any other light in order to illumine itself;
Knowledge (Pure Consciousness)
does not require any other knowledge
except that which is its own nature
in order to be known.

55.   Just as one light does not depend
on another in order to be revealed,
so, what is one's own nature
does not depend on anything else.
(Being of the nature of consciousness
the Self does not require
another consciousness to be known.)

56.   Just as there is no day or night
in the sun as it is of the nature of light only,
so, there is no knowledge or ignorance
in the Self which is of the nature of
Pure Consciousness only.

57.   Just as light assumes the forms
of objects revealed by it,
but is really different from them
though apparently mixed up with them,
so, the Self is different from
the mental modifications.

58.   The Seer is different from the seen
i.e., that which feels pain.
The Self is free from pain.
The Self is the Seer.

59.   One becomes unhappy when
one identifies oneself with the intellect
which has assumed the form
of unhappiness
but not by merely seeing it.

60.   Transmigratory existence
consists of the waking and dream states.
Their root is deep sleep
consisting of ignorance.
No one of these three states
has a real existence
because each goes out of existence
when another arrives.

61.   The Self is pure
and is of a nature contrary
to that which is superimposed.

62.   The Self has no change of states.
The Self is of a changeless nature.

63.   There is no bondage in the Self.
There is no change of condition in the Self.

64.   Bondage is nothing but a delusion
of the intellect;
the removal of this delusion is liberation.

65.   Illumined by the light of the Self
which is Pure Consciousness,
the intellect (falsely) believes
that it is itself conscious.
This is delusion.
This delusion is in the intellect.

66.   Failure to discern the difference
between the intellect and the eternal Self
which is of the nature of Consciousness
creates transmigratory existence.

67.   Having attained
the extremely pure non-dual Knowledge
which is Its own Witness
and contrary to what is superimposed,
a man becomes free from ignorance
and has eternal peace.

68.   When he acquires this Knowledge
which is the supreme purifier,
a man becomes free
from all merit and demerit
produced by ignorance
and accumulated in many other past lives.

69.   Just as one is free from the ideas
of "me" and "mine"
in respect to others' bodies, so,
one becomes free from the ideas of "me"
and "mine" in respect to one's own body
when one knows the supreme truth.
One becomes immediately liberated
in all respects
upon attaining this very pure Knowledge.

70.   The Self is to be known.
It is beyond everything else knowable
as there exists nothing else except It.
I bow down to that pure, all-knowing One
which is to be known.

71.   I bow down to my teacher
whose words fell (into my ears)
and destroyed ignorance (in me)
like the sun's rays falling on darkness
and destroying it.

72.   There is no other attainment higher
than that of the Self.

73.   The conception of the non-Self
is what is called ignorance,
the destruction of which
is known to be liberation.
This destruction is possible
by means of Knowledge only,
which is incompatible with ignorance.

74.   The entire universe
is really non-existent.
The universe appears to exist
only to a deluded intellect.

75.   Unperceived in deep sleep but
perceived (in the waking and dream states)
only by those who are ignorant,
this entire universe is
an outcome of ignorance
and therefore unreal.

76.   When the mind becomes purified
like a clean mirror,
Knowledge is revealed in it.

77.   The attainment of
the one-pointedness of the mind
and the senses is the best of austerities.
It is superior to all religious duties
and all other austerities.

78.   Just as the reflection
and the heat of the sun, found in water
does not belong to water,
so, Consciousness,
though perceived in the intellect
is not a quality of the intellect.
Consciousness is of a nature
opposite to that of the intellect.

79.   The Self whose Consciousness
never goes out of existence
is called the Seer of seeing when it
illumines that modification of the intellect
which is connected with the eye, and
similarly It is called the Hearer of hearing
(and so on.)
The Unborn One is called
the thinker of thought when It illumines
that modification of the mind
which is independent of external objects.
It is called the knower because
Its power of Consciousness never fails.
The Scripture says,
"The Seeing of the Seer is not destroyed."

80.   Just as a second lamp is not necessary
in order to illumine a lamp, so,
a second consciousness is not necessary
to make known Pure Consciousness
which is the nature of the Self.

81.   The body is not the Self.

82.   The conceptions of "me" and "mine"
with regard to the non-Self, the body etc.,
are due to ignorance
and should be renounced
by means of Self-knowledge.

83. A man of ignorance
reaps the results of those actions done
according to particular desires
followed by particular determinations.

84. When the desires
of a man of Self-knowledge vanish
he becomes immortal.

85. When the Witness is discerned
as different from the intellect etc.,
which are unreal,
the Witness does not identify Itself again
with the gross or the subtle body.

86. I have no knowledge
or ignorance in Me as I am of the nature of
homogenous Consciousness only,
just as there is no day or night in the sun
which is of the nature of light only.

87. The Truthful man
who has renounced everything unreal
does not become bound again when he
knows that he is always Consciousness, the
eternally existing Self devoid of everything.

88. No one is freed from the distress of
this transmigratory existence
simply by understanding
the meaning of the sentence.

89. The Self is Intelligence, Self-effulgent,
the Seer, the Innermost, Existence,
free from actions, directly cognized,
the Witness.

90. Without being connected
with anything and pervading everything
by means of Its reflection the Self is always
of the nature of Knowledge
(Pure Consciousness) Itself.

91. All this non-Self appears to exist
for those people who are not discerning,
but it does not exist at all
for men of Knowledge.

92. It is the indirectly expressed meaning
of the word "I"
viz., the innermost and Self-luminous Self
which is expressed in the teaching,
"Thou art That" (You are That).

93. The Self exists in Its own nature
even before one is taught (the meaning of
the sentence, "Thou art That.")

94. Just as a lamp which reveals things
is different from those things,
so is the knower different
from the things known.

95.   The wrong knowledge
that one is happy or unhappy due to
one's identification with the body etc.,
is surely negated by the right knowledge
that one is Pure Consciousness.

96.   The pain comes to an end when
one has the discriminating knowledge
(that one is the Innermost Self).

97.   The word "Thou" comes to mean
one free from pain
on account of its being used in the same
predicament with the word "That"
which means One eternally devoid of pain.
Similarly, used in the same connection
with the word "Thou"
meaning the Innermost Self
(which is directly known), the word "That"
also comes to mean a thing directly known.

98.   One does not see one's own Self,
the Witness, even though the Self
is detached from the non-Self
and Self-evident,
because one's eyes are covered
by ignorance
and one's intellect is captivated by desires.

99. Accept the Self as Self-evident which means the same thing as Self-knowable. The knowledge of the Innermost Self becomes possible when the ego vanishes.

100. The Witness is known by Itself which is of the nature of consciousness only.

101. As I am the Supreme Eternal One I am always contented and have no desires.

102. Everything created by the mind is non-existent.

103. Reality is never destroyed and unreality is never born. The mind does not exist in the Self. The mind, which appears to have both birth and death, does not exist.

104. There is no one who belongs to me nor is there anyone to whom I belong because I am one without a second. The world does not exist.

105. The Self is not within the scope of words.

106. The knowledge of the Self
which is the same in all conditions
is always of the nature of
Self-effulgent Consciousness
and free from duality.

107. False notions cannot be negated
in any way other than knowing the Self.
It is these wrong notions
that are the cause of delusion.
These notions, bereft of their cause,
come to an absolute end,
like fire bereft of fuel
(when Self-knowledge is achieved).

108. I take shelter in the infinite Self,
who is absolute
existence-consciousness-bliss
and who is beyond thought
and expression.

FOUR AIDS TO REALIZATION

109. The great sages say
that there are four aids to realization.
Where they are found in plentitude
liberation is attained.

110. Of these, the first is discrimination
between what is eternal
and what is not eternal.
The second is the lack of attachment
for the objects of enjoyment
that may be gained here or hereafter.
The six noble qualities,
such as calmness of mind
when grouped together
form the third aid to realization.
The fourth and final aid to realization
is the desire for liberation.

DISCRIMINATION

111.   Whatever consists of parts and whole
is not the eternal.
To consider any particular object
to be eternal
would be an error of the imagination.

112.   To distinguish between that which is
eternal and that which is not eternal
is known as "discrimination"
(discernment).

113.   All possessions that may be gained
either here or hereafter
are by their very nature transient
and are of no lasting value.
Not to feel any yearning for them
is known as "non-attachment."

114.   As a consequence of practicing
discrimination between what is eternal
and what is not,
there arises an absence of desire.
This desirelessness is felt
towards all transient objects.

115. The culmination of desirelessness is
attained when one turns away with disgust
from all the objects of desire,
as though they were as abominable
as the excrement of a crow.
The wise say that this feeling comes
as a result of the perception of the defects
that are inherent in
all the objects of enjoyment.

116. The objects of enjoyment
seem attractive to the ignorant.
The wise know that
the objects of enjoyment are worthless.

DISPASSION

117. If one should become blinded by lust,
even the picture of a woman, unreal as it is,
is enough to cause delusion.

118. The man who is deluded
imagines that the brief interval
between two successive periods of pain
is full of bliss.

119. That person who is intelligent
and wise,
and who knows what defects lie hidden
in the objects of enjoyment,
knows how to free himself
from the bonds of desire.

120. Let me tell you
what that subtle path is by means of which
all those who are virtuous
might conquer desire.
The simplest means of conquering desire is
to give up the idea
that a particular object is attractive,
and not to think of it at all.

121. Even when one hears
of a particular object or sees it
no one ever desires to possess it
unless there arises the idea
that it is a desirable object.

122. That mental concept
that a particular object is attractive
is the source of all desires.
Where no such thought arises,
there is no desire.

123. Let him who is intent upon
the conquest of desire
first erase from his mind all ideas
as to the desirability of any given object.

124. Let him who is intent upon
the conquest of desire
give up the feeling of pleasurableness
associated with such objects.

125. Where, as a result of right knowledge
in relation to things
and as a result of reflection,
one becomes aware of
the harm that results,
there does not arise the idea
that a given object is attractive.

126. The conquest of desire
becomes possible,
when as a result of right knowledge,
one becomes aware of
the evil consequences that flow
from the objects of desire.

WEALTH

127. Fear, ever-increasing sorrow,
ego-glorification, discord among friends;
these are some of the evil consequences
that flow from wealth.
Wealth is also a hindrance
to the practice of virtue.
Although the miser worships wealth,
it is not conducive either to salvation
or to self-purification.

128. Wealth makes a person
feel afraid of thieves.
Wealth is attended with fear.
Wealth is a source of discord.
The virtuous never hope to find
any happiness in wealth.

129. Wealth is a source of grief,
both when it is being earned
and when it is preserved.
Wealth is also a source of grief
when it is spent or given as a gift.
Wealth is never a source of bliss.

130. Even the virtuous become greedy
when they begin to acquire wealth.
One who is greedy becomes incapable of
discriminating between good and evil.
One who lacks discrimination is destroyed.

131. The person who is not rich
is victimized by poverty.
The rich are victimized by greed. In either
case wealth is always a source of sorrow.
Wealth is never a source
of permanent happiness.

132. The deluded man
who is lured by the demon of greed
firmly persuades himself
that wealth is a source of happiness.
Lapped in wealth
he falls deeper into delusion.

133. Wealth tends to narrow one's vision.
As he is surrounded by flatterers,
the rich man traverses a path
which the wise have abandoned.
The rich man stumbles into hidden pitfalls.

134. Greed, anger, pride,
conceit and jealousy grow ever more
with the acquisition of wealth.

135. Wealth is ever attended with grief.
None may attain by means of wealth
the highest reward of life.
The wise flee the world.
The wise give up the love of wealth
because wealth is an obstacle in the path.
The wise resort to a life of seclusion.

136. To those blessed ones whose
meritorious deeds have destroyed all sins,
who study the scriptures,
who make use of the power of reason
to discriminate again and again
between the eternal and the transient,
who are endowed with
detachment of a high order
as a result of such discrimination,
and who are ever intent on liberation,
who are self-possessed and enlightened;
with one stroke of dispassion it becomes
easy to cut off all the bonds of life.

137. There are three big gateways
which lead to the sorrowful cycle
of birth and death.
They are lust, greed and the palate:
and all of them lead to death.

138. Out of discrimination
comes dispassion.
The wise say that dispassion
is the root of liberation.
The discriminating person
who desires liberation
should put forth all effort
and acquire dispassion.

139. Tranquility, the control of the senses,
fortitude, renunciation,
faith and concentration of mind
are the six cardinal virtues of life.

TRANQUILITY

140. The wise say that tranquility
comes as a result of
the mind being one-pointed
and being constantly directed
to the object of meditation.

141. That state of mind which enjoys
the nature of the supreme Reality,
and which lies beyond the mind
and its modifications,
is the highest form of tranquility.
That tranquility is blissful.

142. The continuous series
of modifications of the mind,
directed in spite of distraction,
towards the pure consciousness
of the Absolute
is regarded as tranquility
of the middling order.

143. Tranquility may be realized
when its auxiliaries are present.
Its prior auxiliary is intense dispassion.
Its posterior auxiliary consists of
the control of the senses.

144. Non-injury means abstaining from
inflicting pain upon other living beings,
either in thought, expression or action.
Non-injury also includes
regarding all beings as oneself
in thought, word and deed.

145. Compassion means kindness.

146. Dispassion means
the total absence of desire
towards all objects of enjoyment.

147. Internal cleanliness or purity
is attained only by means of
the removal of ignorance.
Where there is inner purity,
mere external cleanliness
becomes less significant.

148. Praying too much in public places
or indulging in elaborate ritualistic worship
where many are gathered,
without having true knowledge,
is mere vanity and ostentation.

149. One should give up
the idea of "I and mine"
in relation to one's physical body.
That is the essence of non-attachment.
Non-attachment is an aid to liberation.

150. One should give up all conceit.
The absence of egotism
includes giving up all pride,
including pride due to one's book learning,
wealth, the practice of spiritual austerity,
having good looks, a noble lineage
or a high station in life.

151. The absence of ego-glorification
includes regarding public opinion
and one's social status with indifference.

152. After having realized
that a crowded place is the least conducive
to the practice of contemplation,
to resort to a sequestered place,
in order to meditate,
is known as the love of solitude.

153. The strong feeling to end
as early as possible
one's bondage to the world
is a characteristic feature
of one who desires liberation.

154. When the senses pursue
the objects of desire,
that pursuit acts upon the mind
like a wind that fans a flame.

155. When the senses are held under
restraint, the mind ceases to be agitated.
The mind then regains its real nature
and attains tranquility.
When the mind is serene
liberation may be attained.

156. Serenity comes as a result of
the control of the senses.
Where self-control has a firm base,
the desire for the objects of enjoyment
does not arise.

157. The purified mind
freed from all inherent defects
attains the supreme peace step by step.

158. When all the defects of the mind
have been overcome by
the practice of self-restraint,
peace soon follows.

FORTITUDE

159. It is as the result of one's past actions
now bearing fruit
that one is called upon to suffer
the threefold ills of life.
To endure them without complaining and
without taking them to heart is fortitude.

160. To the seeker after liberation
there is no armor stronger than fortitude.
Like a well-armed hero
who overcomes all obstacles,
he who is protected by fortitude
overcomes the veil that hides reality.

161. Those who are endowed with
fortitude may attain the goal of yoga.
Those who are not endowed with fortitude
are overpowered by obstacles
and they drift about
like withered leaves before the wind.

162. The aspirant after liberation
should attain fortitude in full measure.
The attainment of fortitude is facilitated by
the earnest desire for liberation
and by intense dispassion.

163. By the practice of fortitude
one should conquer sorrow.

RENUNCIATION

164. When as a result of
the intense desire for liberation,
one feels no interest whatever
in worldly things,
that very day the intelligent aspirant
becomes fit for renunciation.

165. The term "renunciation" implies
the giving up of all those actions
which one had previously imagined
to be a source of happiness.

166. In its primary meaning renunciation
implies the giving up of the objects
which influence the mind.

167. In order to attain the main objective
one should make use of
the requisite means to it,
for in the absence of the means,
the goal cannot be achieved.

168. Renunciation without dispassion
is of no avail.

169. Without faith there is no exertion,
and without exertion
there is no achievement.
Hence it is that
those who are devoid of faith
remain lost in the sorrowful ocean
of the cycle of birth and death.

CONCENTRATION

170. It is only by virtue of concentration
that it becomes possible
for one to attain one's goal.

171. As an aid to the attainment of
the supreme peace,
concentration stands unexcelled.
At no time can the aspirant after liberation
afford to dispense with concentration.

172. Where there is
the most intense form of dispassion,
and where there is
the supreme love of liberation,
it is by virtue of their combined influence
that one attains concentration of mind.

THE DESIRE FOR LIBERATION

173. The love of liberation
lies at the root of realization.

174. There are four classes of aspirants.
They may be classified as the very eager,
the moderately eager, the lukewarm
and the indifferent.

175. The feeling which impels one
to go through the travail of the world here,
and willingly renounce everything,
be it pleasure or pain,
is a characteristic feature of the most
ardent type of the love of liberation.

176. "There is a time for liberation.
What is the use of being in a hurry?
I will think of liberation at leisure,
sometime in the distant future,
after I have finished all my duties,
and have had my fill of enjoyment."
Such an attitude of mind
shows a weak desire for liberation.

177. "Just as a lucky wayfarer
might find by chance a precious stone,
if I can have liberation by a lucky accident,
I will feel happy." Such is the attitude of
mind of the weakest aspirant.

178. One who is pure of heart
becomes capable of discriminating
between right and wrong.
Such a person is devoid of the craving
for sense-pleasures,
is aware of the difference between
what is eternal and what is not eternal,
and is ever intent upon final liberation.

179. One who is endowed
with the strongest desire for liberation
is liberated in this lifetime.

180. It is essential
that one should try repeatedly
until one frees oneself from within.

181. An intense love of liberation
is the culmination of all spiritual discipline.
The discipline that we often note
in those lacking the desire for liberation
is merely for pleasing the public.

182. The desire for liberation grows
in growing measure
from the discrimination
between the eternal and the non-eternal,
and from the awareness of
the transient nature of life,
and from the fear of death,
and from knowledge of the ills of life.

SUPERIMPOSITION

183. You say that you are subject to
birth and death, sorrow and suffering,
ill-health and old age. But really speaking,
they are not inherent in your real nature.
They are but figments of the mind.
Seek your real nature as the Self
and give up this delusion.

184. All your grief is in vain.
Your grief is the product of fear.
Give up this error
and become calm of mind.

185. You have superimposed
the idea of death upon the Self
and out of delusion you imagine that you
are subject to birth and death.
Do not grieve because
birth and death are not natural to you.
Birth and death are unreal.

186. All that you have said
in a state of delusion is unreal.

187. To attribute to that which is real the
nature or the properties of unreal objects
is known as superimposition.
It is as though one imagines
that a wayside rope is a snake.

188. Ignorance is the cause of
the world seeming to be real.
Ignorance is something different
from Reality.

189. Ignorance is the cause
of all unreal superimpositions.

190. Impelled by tendencies
accumulated from the past,
the embodied being takes part
in various kinds of activities.
Some of these are wise
and the others are not wise.
As a result one enjoys pleasure,
or suffers pain
both in this world and in the next.

191. It is in this way that
the embodied being becomes lost
in the cyclic changes of repeated births
and deaths.

192. It is by means of the mind
that one is drawn towards
the world of external objects,
or knows all that takes place
either within oneself, or outside.
It is by means of the mind that one smells,
sees, speaks, touches, eats and acts.

193. Bondage and liberation
are also of the mind.
A pure mind is the cause of liberation, but
an impure mind is the cause of bondage.
That which is good
comes out of discrimination.
That which is evil comes out of
the lack of discrimination.

194. When it becomes tainted
by the activities that are born of desire,
the individual loses its freedom
and becomes distracted and distressed.

195. Let the aspirant keep his mind pure,
so that it may be favorable
to the achievement of progress.

196. By thinking about the various ills
of life, from birth to old age and death,
and by thinking about how life is subject to
disease here and suffering hereafter,
he who is wise should renounce
all binding desires.

197. Where the divine virtues
are practiced,
where the demonic vices are eschewed,
where the attainment of liberation
is the sole aim,
it is there that the mind attains tranquility.

198. Where there is no coveting
the wealth of others,
where there is neither deception
nor calumny,
where all lustful thoughts
have been laid aside,
it is there that the mind attains tranquility.

199. The food which is too bitter,
salty or sour should be eschewed.
Also food which is overly pungent, hot,
causing irritation or has turned stale
should be avoided.
By avoiding such foods purity is developed.

200. He who takes food that is nutritious,
and in moderate quantity,
who is ever fond of solitude,
who speaks to the point
and says only that which is beneficent
and who is self-restrained
soon attains tranquility of mind.

201. Where there is tranquility,
liberation is near.
Strive earnestly to attain
tranquility of mind
by means of self-control.

202. In reality, the Self is
the pure witnessing consciousness.
The Self is neither the doer of actions
nor is it the enjoyer of the fruits of actions.

203. In relation to
the various activities of life
which are performed through
the physical body,
pure consciousness remains unaffected.
This is similar to the sun
remaining unaffected
by the various activities
that occur in the world.

204. Those who do not know the supreme
truth, whose minds are clouded by illusion,
tend to superimpose upon the supreme Self
the idea that the Self is the doer.
It is not the Self that is the doer;
it is something else.

205. Where there is no right knowledge,
when people do not realize
that the Self is pure consciousness,
ever unattached,
they attribute to the Self
whatever actions are performed
by that which is other than the Self.

206. The pure consciousness is one
and indivisible.

207. The pure consciousness permeates
the entire world of manifestation.
The pure consciousness
ever remains what it is,
the unborn and unmanifest,
without beginning and without end.

208. The Self is pure consciousness.
The Self undergoes no change.
In itself the Self is the knower.

209. The Self,
which is the innermost Self of all,
is Self-effulgent, devoid of parts,
unattached, pure and not subject to any
kind of modification.
The Self is eternal bliss.
It is the witnessing Self
that is the source of all consciousness.
The Self is indivisible
and free from all adjuncts.

210. The Self is not subject to birth,
growth, death or dissolution.
The Self is our inmost nature.

211. People superimpose the Self
upon that which is not the Self,
and conversely they superimpose
that which is not the Self upon the Self.
That is why, from erroneous knowledge,
they become subject to the bondage of
the cycle of births and deaths.

212. It is as a result
of such superimposition
that wrong ideas come to prevail.
It is then that one erroneously thinks
of oneself to be a human being.

213. It is on account of
the defect of the intellect
that one wrongly superimposes the ideas of
birth, old age, death, thirst, fear, pleasure
and pain upon the Self.
All these are characteristics
of that which is not the Self.
The nature of the Self is entirely different.

214. The Self shines
by the light of its own consciousness.
When the intellect becomes
extremely pure and transparent, its nature
is similar to the nature of the Self.
By virtue of its proximity
to the innermost Self
the intellect catches the light of the Self.
This is similar to how
a crystal reflects the light of the sun.

215. Ignorant people mistake the intellect
for the Self.

216. The moment something
which is other than the Self
is mistaken for the Self,
a chain reaction takes place.
Every act of superimposition
becomes in turn
the cause of the next superimposition
in the series.

217. When the pure nature of the Self
becomes hidden
by the veiling power of illusion,
out of the resultant delusion
people superimpose the idea of the one Self
upon all those things that are not the Self.
People then mistakenly adopt the view
towards those things
which are not the Self: "I am these things."

218. Just as one tends to superimpose
the idea of the Self upon a body in a dream,
similarly in the waking state also
one superimposes upon the Self
diverse concepts such as birth, death,
hunger, fear, thirst and pain
although in reality
none of these are attributes of the Self.

219. When one is propelled
by the power of projection,
one superimposes upon the Self
various kinds of activities
and as a result experiences consequences
that flow from those activities
such as good and evil.
This is how people wander about
lost in the sea of births and deaths.

220. On account of the evil consequences
that flow from superimposition,
one imagines that the Self is bound
by earth-born ties such as birth, death,
hardship and hunger.

221. It is this mistaken notion
of regarding that which is not the Self
as though it were the Self
that lies at the basis of all superimposition
and it is the origin of the delusion
to which all human beings are subject.
It is also the cause of
the cycle of births and deaths.

222. It is this superimposition
of that which is not the Self upon the Self
which is the cause
of all mundane existence.
When the superimposition ceases,
the cycle of births and deaths also ceases.

223. The cycle of births and deaths
is dependent upon superimposition
for its seeming existence.
Those who are bound
continue to experience
the cycle of births and deaths.
Those who are free
do not continue to experience
the cycle of births and deaths.

224. Action binds. Renunciation liberates.

225. Ignorance is the cause
of superimposition.
Ignorance has no being.
Ignorance is unreal.
Even though it is non-existent,
it creates the illusion of
the cycle of births and deaths.
That is why the analogy of the rope
that is mistaken for a snake
is so appropriate.

226. As a result of superimposition
the individual becomes subject to sorrow
and suffering.

227. Delusion is caused by
superimposition.
Delusion veils from oneself
one's own real nature.

228. By knowledge alone
may ignorance be destroyed.
Ignorance cannot be destroyed by action
because action is not opposed to ignorance.

229. As a result of action,
individuals appear to be born
and appear to be destroyed.
It is in this way that
the vicious cycle of birth and death goes on.

230. Action is the product of ignorance.
Action flourishes by means of ignorance.

231. The Self is
the witnessing consciousness.
The Self is the eternal "I am."

232. By virtue of its radiant light
the sun illumines all objects under it.
Inert matter does not illumine the sun.
Similar is the case with the Self.
The Self is pure consciousness.
The Self illumines the intellect
as well as all that the intellect surveys.

233. The sun is not in need
of any other light,
either to make itself known
or to reveal other objects.
Similarly the consciousness
that is inherent in the Self
makes itself known
as the "I" consciousness in individuals.

TEMPORARY HAPPINESS

OR

ETERNAL BLISS

234. Bliss is natural to the Self.

235. There is a limit to the love
of the various things that people imagine
confer happiness upon them.
There is no limit to the love of the Self.

236. Out of all of that which is desirable,
ones own Self is the dearest.

237. Supreme bliss is inherent in the Self.
Whoever substitutes for the Self
anything else as the object of his quest
after happiness merely pursues pain.

238. People do not know that happiness
is inherent in the Self.
People do not know the real nature
of the Self.
That is why people fondly pursue
external objects.
Pursuing external objects
is not the way of the wise.

239. People do not know
that all these objects
are really sources of misery.
People have forgotten
the blissful nature of the Self.
It is a result of their ignorance
that people pursue pleasure,
and go in search of external objects.
People who pursue pleasure
and go in search of external objects
are pursuing pain without realizing that
they are pursuing pain.

240. All those who identify
with their physical bodies
tend to seek happiness in external things.
They think about them,
go in quest of them, and wish to have them,
because they mistakenly imagine that
happiness is inherent in external objects.

241. The happiness that is derived
from external sources
is always mingled with sorrow.
There is sorrow at the time of enjoyment,
and there is greater sorrow
when the enjoyment comes to an end.

242. The happiness
that is derived from external objects
is always coupled with pain,
both at the time of enjoyment
and when the happiness comes to an end.

243. The Self is bliss itself
and the bliss of the Self lasts forever.
There is nothing similar to
the bliss of the Self.
The bliss of the Self is full, eternal, unique
and free from fear.

244. The Self can be known immediately.
The Self is ever present.
On account of ignorance,
and on account of the combination of
the body and the senses,
people do not know the Self
either in the waking state
or in the dream state.

245. The Self is
existence-consciousness-bliss.

THE WORLD IS NOT REAL

246. The Self is the One without a second.
The Self is unique in nature.
The Self is the only reality.
The world is not real.

247. When the apparent reality
of the world is removed,
all that remains is pure Being.

248. Similar to how
as a result of defective vision
the one moon seems to be two moons,
as a result of the defective comprehension
of the intellect
the One Reality seems to be multifarious.
When the illusion of the intellect
is conquered
the One Reality reasserts itself
and makes itself manifest.

249. Space is ever the same,
irrespective of the presence or absence
of the pot which seems to divide space.
It is similar with the supreme Reality.

250. It is only in the imagination
of the foolish that space universal
seems to be cut into fragments.

251. Examination reveals to us that
all the adjuncts (superimposed on the Self)
and their characteristics,
which are the source of separateness,
are entirely unreal.
The adjuncts and their characteristics are
the products of the delusion of the intellect.
They have no being; and they fade away
upon awakening to the Reality.
This is similar to how
the objects of the dream world
fade away upon awakening.

252. Both the waking state
and the dreaming state
are subject to the illusion
which the intellect imposes upon us.
The waking state is unreal
and the dream state is unreal.

253. Both the waking state
and the dream state
are products of our ignorance.

254. In the deep sleep state
both the waking state
and dreaming state cease.

255. The absolute Reality is ever-existent,
non-dual,
and not subject to any kind of change.

256. That Supreme Truth,
the One ultimate Reality,
it is That which is of the nature of
existence, consciousness and bliss.

257. You are not the physical body,
nor the vital force, nor the sense organs,
nor the mind, nor the intellect, nor the ego.
You are not any of these,
either individually or collectively.
That supreme witnessing consciousness,
that pure resplendent Being, you are That.

258. Only that which is born
can in succession undergo
the process of growth and decay, and also
come to an end in the course of time.
That which is devoid of birth
is also devoid of death.
That eternal unborn Self, you are That.

259. It is the physical body
which is liable to be born,
and that alone is also subject to death.
Hence it is that
the physical body is dissolved
when the fruit of karma is exhausted.
As for you,
you are the witnessing consciousness
which continues to survive
regardless of all the seeming changes
such as the birth or death of a body.
The Self remains what it is
and is not subject to any kind of change.

260. It is the absolute pure consciousness
which illumines all things
both when we are in the waking state
and when we are dreaming.
The Self makes itself manifest
in every individual as the I-consciousness
and remains unchanged
through every modification of the intellect.
That absolute pure consciousness,
you are That.

261. The Absolute Reality is ever present
in the pure hearts of those who are
absorbed in the deepest concentration.
Such persons are ever awake to the reality
of the witnessing consciousness,
and they are always absorbed
in the transcendent bliss of that Reality.

262. By superimposing
upon pure consciousness
the attributes of an individual,
you imagine that you have become
an embodied being.
Such is not the case;
you are in reality the unborn Self.

263. That infinite truth,
that eternal pure consciousness,
you are That.

264. That eternal bliss
knows no division within itself,
for it is homogeneous in nature.
It is not a product of action;
for it always remains unmodified by action.
That is the Self of us all.
That supreme, unmanifest,
pure consciousness,
you are That.

PRACTICE MEDITATION

UNCEASINGLY

265. Be ever absorbed in meditating upon
that which never changes,
which is eternal,
and which lies beyond all activity.

266. When the limiting adjuncts
are no longer superimposed on the Self all
that remains is the one pure consciousness.

267. The mind should be wholly absorbed
in the consciousness of the Self.
The mind should be permeated
by the consciousness of the Self.

268. One who desires to attain liberation
should practice meditation unceasingly,
until all the wrong ideas
that arise in the mind
as to the nature of the Self
are completely eradicated.

269. When all the wrong ideas
have come to an end,
there are no more obstacles
to the attainment of the highest knowledge.
In this way eternal bliss is realized.

270. One should identify oneself
with the Self, the seer,
who does not engage in any kind of activity.

271. One comes to identify oneself
with the witnessing consciousness.

272. One knows oneself thus:
"I am neither the body, nor the vital force,
nor the sense organs, nor the ego,
nor the mind, nor the intellect;
I am the eternal
inmost witnessing consciousness and
I am not any of the changing phenomena."

273. "I am neither fat nor lean,
neither a child, nor a youth,
nor an old person.
The inmost witnessing consciousness –
that I am."

274. I am not limited either by the body,
or the sense organs, or the intellect.
Old age, death, hunger, thirst, grief
and delusion, all these are far from me.
I am pure consciousness, the ever-free.

275. I am neither the hands nor the feet,
neither the organ of speech nor the eyes,
neither the vital force nor the mind,
nor the intellect.
I am similar to universal space,
I am that which is all-pervading,
the unchanging pure consciousness.

276. The word liberation means
freedom from the bondage of ignorance.
In itself liberation means
the awareness of the Self
and this may be realized only by means of
the deepest concentration.

277. It is neither by
the clothes that one wears,
nor by the language that one speaks,
that anyone can attain liberation.
Liberation lies in being established
in the Self,
which is indivisible and conscious.
One must give up the ideas of 'I and mine'
and be established in the Self
in order to realize the Self.

278. The aspirant after liberation
should always be devoted to the Self.

279. I am the pure, inmost Self,
untouched by ignorance, and ever existent.
I am tranquil and limitless.
I am an ocean of eternal bliss.

280. I am free from illusion.
I am free from all of the effects of illusion.
I am the witnessing consciousness.

281. I am neither the effect
nor the cause of anything.
Within me and around me
there is nothing other than the infinite Self.
I have no old age, decay or death.
I am imperishable. I am eternal bliss.
I am one without a second.

282. Where the mind functions no longer,
where there are no objects of knowledge,
and where the Self,
the witnessing consciousness,
is the sole reality,
there arises the experience of awakening
into the deepest state
of natural concentration.

283. It is certain that
one who is solely intent upon
the realization of the eternal Reality
in the deepest state
of natural concentration
becomes the eternal Reality
and the vicious cycle of birth and death
comes to an end.
Such a one attains
the eternal changeless continuous bliss
that knows no obstacles.

284. Rare are the knowers
of the absolute Reality.
The knowers of the absolute Reality
are the absolute Reality.
They are not conscious of anything within
them such as the idea of "I and mine";
nor are they conscious of anything
outside them such as "this or that."
They are lost in the infinite ocean of bliss,
which is the bliss of the inmost Self,
and they remain forever absorbed
in the Great Silence.

285. They are the most fortunate
who have lost their individuality
in that Supreme Being.
They alone are liberated,
even though the liberated might seem to be
embodied beings
from the viewpoint of those
who are not liberated.

286. While engaged
in the practice of concentration,
the aspirant after liberation
should be on guard against being careless.

287. The wise should not abstain from
the pursuit of the knowledge of the Self
even for a moment.

288. It is in the deepest concentration that
all the knots of the heart are cut asunder.
These knots of the heart
are compact forms of desire,
and ideas such as "I and mine."
They are the sources of unreal knowledge.
When they are cut asunder,
one's bondage to the past comes to an end.

289. Be ever more intent
upon practicing the deepest concentration.
Burn up all the obstacles
that are caused by delusion.
Take your fill of delight
in the bliss of the eternal,
which is the nectar of immortality.

290. It is only in the deepest concentration
that all the ripples of thought
that arise in the mind are stilled
and there reigns complete tranquility.

291. To withdraw the mind
from all the objects of knowledge,
and to cease to identify oneself with them
by making the mind merge
in pure consciousness
is known as pratyahara.
Every aspirant after liberation
should diligently practice pratyahara.

292. With his senses made tranquil, with
his mind controlled and body motionless,
the disciple sat somewhere,
and devoted himself exclusively
to the pursuit of the Self.

LIBERATION

293. I have realized eternal bliss.
I am the infinite, innermost Self,
which is all-pervading, taintless and pure.

294. I am neither the doer, nor the enjoyer
of the fruits of action. I know no change.
I am not the product of any kind of activity.
I am bliss. I am the Self,
the one without a second,
the ever-auspicious.

295. I have attained the knowledge
of the imperishable Self,
and realized its inherent glory
and indivisible bliss.

296. I am one with
that witnessing consciousness.

297. I am that pure consciousness
which is untainted
and which remains unchanged.

298. That person who is devoid of the
consciousness of the body and the mind,
who knows the supreme Reality
and the supreme bliss is liberated in life.

299. One who has gone beyond
the reach of thought,
is free from the consciousness of the body,
and who has gained
the supreme knowledge by direct intuition,
is indeed liberated.

300. The Self has neither form nor shape.
To know that
and to identify oneself with the Self
is to go beyond the state
of an embodied being.

SRI SANKARA'S

NINE KEYS TO SELF REALIZATION

1. *Discrimination between the eternal and the temporary.*

2. *Dispassion.*

3. *Peace or Restfulness.*

4. *Self Control.*

5. *Renunciation.*

6. *Endurance or Fortitude.*

7. *Faith.*

8. *Self Abidance.*

9. *The Desire for Liberation.*

Sri Sankara grouped numbers 3 through 8 above together (the six qualities).

Please use the contact form at seeseer.com to let us know if reading Powerful Quotes from Sankara was a good experience for you.

Other books published by The Freedom Religion Press that you may be interested in are:

1. The Crest Jewel of Wisdom and other writings of Sankaracharya translated by Charles Johnston.

2. The Seven Steps to Awakening by Ramana Maharshi, Nisargadatta Maharaj, Sankara, Vasistha, Annamalai Swami, Muruganar and Sadhu Om.

3. Three Hundred Quotes from Hinduism from more than forty sources.

4. Developing Spiritual Consciousness Second Abridged Edition by Swami Mukerji.

5. The Crest Jewel of Discrimination by Sankara. Translated by John Richards.

For information about these and other spiritual books go to: www.seeseer.com